CONFLUENCE POINT

CENTRIST SOLUTIONS TO AMERICA'S MONUMENTAL QUAGMIRES

I0437033

RALPH NWOBI

DENVER, COLORADO

*This book is dedicated to all Americans who
want a smaller, more efficient government
and elevated political discourse.*

Table of Contents

PROLOGUE

There is nothing wrong with America that cannot be fixed by what is right with America.

So said the man from Hope, Arkansas.

I believe this to be true and this is part of my motivation for writing this book. I have heard people say that America is on a decline because of all the challenges that we face, both domestic and abroad.

I opine that these pundits are wrong. America's best days are still ahead of us. The uniqueness and exceptionalism of this country are not concepts merely talked about in the media. It is an integral part of who we are as a people, and also who we should aspire to be...great people from a great nation, destined to lead the free world.

To achieve this, we have to make sincere efforts to solve our problems. In our two-party system, there cannot be sincerity of effort if we do not try to compromise. The very nature of our democracy requires that compromises should always be made when necessary.

Being an ideologue or an extremist should never be celebrated. Visceral convictions that are not supported by facts should never be encouraged. To compromise does not mean that one side will totally abandon its values or principles for the views of others. It just means that one side can negotiate with the other side with an open and receptive mind.

An open mind must be flexible and willing to look at issues from the other side's perspective to understand where they are coming from. Politicians can disagree without being disagreeable. They can have policy disagreements without using hyperbolic or polarizing rhetoric to tear down their opponents.

Theodore Roosevelt once said that a typical vice of American politics is the avoidance of saying something real on real issues. We have to correct this trend. Our elected officials and politicians from both parties have to get real by coming together to solve problems.

If both sides can be willing to do this, then they will be able to easily solve the national problems that everybody agrees on. For instance, both Republicans and Democrats agree that our education system needs some fixing. Common sense measures to address this problem should not be met with unnecessary difficulty or gridlock because of partisan differences.

For problems that are complex, more patience,

explanation and listening are required, and individual politicians must become more informed. It requires more openness, flexibility and a willingness to move an inch or more from one's position, so as to meet at a mutually agreeable point--the middle ground. That is the point at which most big feats can be achieved by both parties.

I call that the confluence point. That is compromise...and it does not show weakness!

The essence of our democracy... the ethos of the democratic process, requires that the two sides find common ground on which to solve problems. They ought to function synergistically to get better results.

Compromise is a word that has to be encouraged in our political parlance. There has to be a paradigm shift in the way we engage in politics today. We have to get the politics right in order to get the policies right.

That is my other motivation for writing this book.

1

EDUCATION

The need for improvement in our nation's education system is widely acknowledged. America's ranking in education has declined when compared to that of most developed countries. The aim should be for the United States to get back on top. Having taught in public schools, I have experienced these problems first hand. We spend the most money in education, more than most countries, but we do not get the best value for the taxpayer dollars spent.

The notion that we can continue spending a lot of money on education without making structural changes and still expect to get wonderful results is a non sequitur.

Democrats and Republicans understand this. We all have children that attend school, thus both parties should be able to come together and embrace common sense measures that can improve our educational system. Some of the measures are:

First, great teachers must be rewarded. At every government level, there should be a reward system set up to reward teachers that are highly motivated and really take their jobs seriously. These kinds of programs will increase the morale of these great teachers, challenge the teachers that are doing their work perfunctorily, and send a strong signal to the sub-par teachers that there could be consequences for inadequate performance.

Second, the termination of the employment of teachers should not be so difficult or highly impracticable. Teachers have to understand that they are accountable to their superior colleagues who have certain powers, including recommending certain disciplinary actions against the teacher.

Of course, these powers should not be abused or used in an arbitrary and capricious manner against a teacher. The bottom line is that it should be reasonable and possible to fire a poor quality teacher for good cause, just like in other jobs.

Third, we should implement programs that promote early childhood education across the board. Pre-Kindergarten programs are vital for all children, but especially for the most vulnerable, including children from economically-disadvantaged homes, minority children and children from households where a language other than English is spoken. The minds of young school kids have to be captured early, in order to ensure greater academic success in the future.

Third grade is another particularly important transitional stage in a child's education. This is the grade at which children stop learning to read and start reading to learn. It is a critical period in which children gain foundational skills such as phonemic awareness, phonics and basic vocabulary that will enable them to later access text in order to read for meaning. Thus, programs at that stage that improve early literacy skills, for example, should be adopted and implemented for all students, despite their background.

Fourth, school programs in science should be emphasized more. America ranks in the twenties in math and science among the industrialized countries of the world. We ought to be at the top. This is very necessary because we need to be able to compete globally as the world gets more digitized and technologically advanced.

Fifth, discipline should be restored to the classroom. There is an obvious correlation between children that are disciplined and respectful, and increased academic performance. The aim here should not be to give license to be unnecessarily punitive to students, but it should be to give teachers more powers to enable them to control the students and manage the classrooms better.

Enforcing school rules and regulations in schools will also equip our students with coping mechanisms and adequate problem solving skills that will enable them to excel and thrive in a tough, uncertain and unpredictable world. This is better than producing over-protected and hypersensitive kids that find it difficult to deal with constructive criticism. There should be greater emphasis on emotional intelligence than just academic excellence. This is perhaps the greatest gift that we can give to our children.

Students should be made to clearly understand that teachers and school administrators are in charge. In my experience teaching in public schools, it seemed that teachers were often made to explain or even in some cases apologize for their interactions with students, especially when they acted in a firm and assertive manner. This trend needs to be changed.

Sixth, we have to reduce the number of students in a classroom. Class size matters. If a class is smaller, a teacher is better able to keep an eye on and adequately monitor individual student activities. He or she will be better able to focus and give account on the progress or even retrogression of any student. Reducing the number of students will involve hiring more qualified teachers.

Emphasis should be placed on the adjective: qualified. We must also ensure that school districts hire teachers that use targeted pedagogical methods and evidence-based techniques for all students. This is important because different students learn in different ways.

We have to use pedagogical methods that maximize the learning potential of each student in every school. Employing teachers that have the adequate credentials, motivation and passion should be a sine qua non to reducing the number of students in classrooms and ultimately fixing the education system.

Seventh, we have to rebuild the infrastructures in the schools. Old school buildings should be modernized and fixed. Avant garde facilities and infrastructures should be placed in the schools. The laboratories should be equipped with state of the art equipment. This will create a wonderful learning environment and effectively put in place the right ambience for a more qualitative assimilation of information.

Eighth, we have to motivate the school children - their morale has to be raised. Kids these days are not sufficiently motivated. It almost seems that since President Kennedy's motivational challenge to Americans to put a man on the moon, we have become really relaxed. Students need to be shown why they should learn, and not just be given materials to study. We have to instill in them the burning desire to thrive academically by giving them something to which to aspire. We have to make reading cool again, in this age of excessive digital takeover of our lives.

Finally, we have to ensure that we hire exceptionally qualified principals to run the schools. School principals are the functional equivalents of ship captains. They should embody the academic pillar and moral compass for each school. They must have conspicuous leadership and management qualities. They should have a clear vision regarding the direction to take the school and a clear plan on how to get there. A principal must lead and must be dependable. He or she also has to be able to listen and defer to teachers in certain unique situations.

In other words, the qualifications required of a principal should be very stringent. It should not be solely based on education or longevity in the system. In a potential school principal, there must exist a passion and a burning desire to transform a school, if necessary, or to take a school's performance to the next level. The aim should be to deliver the highest quality education to our children.

We should not let this crisis in our education system go to waste. It should be seen as an opportunity to revamp the system and put us on the right trajectory to producing the best students in the world. A good educational system will also improve our economy by serving as a means of upward mobility to lift some families out of poverty.

These solutions can be agreed upon by members of both parties. Our elected officials therefore owe it to the country to pass bipartisan legislation at every government level, so as to empower the relevant agencies to embark on these measures.

In the words of Diogenes - The foundation of every state is the education of its youth.

Our strong foundation in the economic strength of this country is inextricably linked to the quality education of our school children. The epistemology of our education has to be reassessed. We owe it to our young ones to adopt middle-of-the-road approaches in meeting the challenges to the country's educational system.

2

FOREIGN POLICY

In an increasingly globalized world there is a greater need now, more than ever, for America's role in the world to be clearly defined. Democrats and Republicans understand this. The rest of the world looks up to America to lead in most world events or incidents. America's economic and military superiority makes us uniquely qualified to continue in this leadership capacity.

However, this does not mean that we have to get involved unnecessarily in any situation, anywhere in the world. America cannot police the rest of the world. We have domestic issues here to also deal with. There is a lot of nation building needed here in the homeland.

Consequently, it presents a difficulty for our leaders to effectively articulate a foreign policy that walks the fine line of not getting unnecessarily involved in the affairs of other countries, yet maintaining our position as the moral compass of the world. The United States is the leading country that will intervene when it is needed and when emergencies arise in other countries.

To that end, some of these solutions should help us in walking this fine line and ironing out this wrinkle that besieges our foreign policy.

First, there should always be clarity of purpose in our mission. This means that before we intervene in any crisis outside the homeland, we have to be very sure about what is happening there and how we are going to engage in the conflict. The duration and manner have to be clearly stated.

Success on the mission has to be defined. Exit strategies also have to be discussed. This whole idea of Democrats being perceived as being dovish and Republicans being perceived as hawkish should not be encouraged. Politicians on both sides of the aisle should adopt policies that make our goals and objectives clear to everybody. This shows certainty and predictability.

The rest of the world will have a greater respect for a predictable and dependable America.

Second, we should not be apologetic in the use of our power, so long as the power is used justifiably. There is no need to apologize for our military might. America spends the most in the world in improving our military might and there should be no hesitation to use this when necessary.

America's military might is such that smart countries

understand and work as America's allies. However, the countries that have policymakers that are unreasonable enough to test America's might, should be made to feel the full impact of what happens when a person intentionally pulls at the tail of a tiger.

Third, America should continue in its current trend of showing respect for the sovereignty of other nations. Every nation likes to be respected and citizens of every nation are also patriotic. No country likes to be told what to do, even if the country knows that America may be a stronger and more influential nation. We can nudge or gently persuade other countries to see things from our perspective, but we should never be seen to be pushy or overly coercive.

This is because such diplomatic moves will trigger the national pride of people with whom we are dealing and will make them less amenable to our requests. America is more respected for the power of our example, rather than the example of our power.

Fourth, we should always ask whether our vital interests are at stake before intervening in foreign disagreements. Purposeful intervention can be implemented if needed, when there is a significant emergency or human disaster. We can take a stand on a matter, but the stance does not necessarily have to cost the taxpayers. We do not have to spend money to express our position on every international dispute that arises. We can act as umpires, perhaps, and not as the self-appointed police of the world.

Fifth, we have to continue the practice of not criticizing our seated presidents on foreign soil. As a corollary to this, politicians and candidates should also be very careful with what they say generally about domestic or international affairs, when they are abroad.

Words matter. They have consequences and words that are uttered by America's public figures and officials can have a significant impact on the world stage.

Sixth, we have to reappraise all the money that we send abroad. There has to be a detailed accounting of such money and we have to know who actually receives such money and whether it is actually used for its intended purpose.

America should not send money to countries that do not have our best interests at heart. Foreign countries should not routinely expect aid from America. There has to be justification for such spending. The money has to buy us something. It has to buy loyalty, at the least, from the receiving countries.

This will also enable us to clearly define and distinguish between our allies, friends and countries with which we have a special relationship.

Finally, we have to be generally careful before we go into wars. We also have to assess situations and figure out whether a war is winnable or not.

For instance, given the intricacies involved in the Afghanistan war, it should be reasonable to conclude that it is an unwinnable war. It is impracticable to believe that we can be in Afghanistan and defeat the Taliban and also do nation building there. Such a project is really cost intensive and not financially feasible.

The Taliban is deeply entrenched there. They will always be there. Afghans will solve the problem of Afghanistan by themselves. Our military can only do what great militaries do…stop bad things from happening. But it cannot be expected to intervene in a foreign country by changing the people's way of life or thinking. We can only do so much.

It is unfathomable that some people believe that all wars are winnable. Jingoism does not solve any problems. There is no need to be unnecessarily doctrinaire about this issue. It should not be a partisan issue.

Continued U.S. military presence there will only serve as a recruiting tool for terrorist organizations. An integral part of being fiscally conservative is endeavoring not to be profligate in our military spending and missions. We should always send our brave men and women only to missions that are economically sustainable and militarily attainable.

Democrats and Republicans can agree on these measures because these are views that represent where most Americans stand on these issues. It is reprehensible and inexcusable for politicians to continue to kick the can down the road on this. This needs to be addressed now.

Americans are war weary and will want soldiers to be put in harm's way only for the worthiest of causes. Many military personnel are coming back with post-traumatic stress disorder and related challenges. We have to focus more on rehabilitating, treating and reintegrating these brave men and women back into civil society.

Congress ought to pass legislation that will make it easier to adopt these solutions.

It should also be noteworthy that we, as a country under President Obama's administration, have done remarkably well in foreign policy. There should be bipartisan support and recognition of these accomplishments and they should continue.

The feats speak for themselves. Some of them are:

1. Eliminating Osama Bin Laden in a methodical and surgical manner, in order to not leave any lingering doubts
2. Bringing the war with Iraq to an end
3. Increasing the use of drones and appropriate counterintelligence and counterinsurgency techniques in the eradication of many terrorists in the world
4. Setting a date for the withdrawal of United States troops from Afghanistan
5. Killing of Somali pirates that attempted to hold a U.S. ship hostage
6. Helping in the removal of Muammar Gaddaffi of Libya, without a loss of any U.S. soldier
7. Supporting the Egyptians in the removal of Mubarak

8. Taking a tough stance with Iran, including the imposition of crippling sanctions
9. Restoring respect and goodwill from other countries, especially Europe, back to the U.S.

These are some of the great achievements that have been accomplished under the Obama administration. These are all good things. I have not met any Democrat or Republican who does not like these things.

These policies should therefore be adopted and continued by elected officials of both parties. There should be a consensus on these solutions and we ought to come to the middle, the confluence point...and continue these policies to improve our foreign policy.

3

CAMPAIGN FINANCE REFORM

It is a generally known fact that the way campaigns are funded should be reformed. Democrats and Republicans agree on that. This huge windfall and sometimes secretive money that enters campaigns now was all made possible because of policies adopted by both sides and because of the Citizens United decision. This Supreme Court ruling essentially held that corporations are people and should be allowed to contribute unlimited amounts of money to political campaigns of their choice.

The ruling equated money to free speech that is protected under the first amendment. Super PACS are also very visible now in our politics. These organizations can now be formed by an individual or individuals. They do not have to expose their identities to the general

public, but only have to meet some continued requirements with the federal electoral commission.

They can run political ads against any candidate or
for any cause. They are expected not to coordinate with
the candidate's campaign directly.

Everybody can easily see the problem this causes.
Now a political ad does not even need to have the
imprimatur of the candidate. The candidate does not
have to be responsible for or accountable to the electorate for an ad with misleading information.

Some of the PACS that put out these ads do not
let facts get in the way when they have a story to tell.
Misinformation and disinformation of the electorate
have become normal in our politics.

Truth is being under-emphasized. It is now relative.
A lot depends now on messaging and propaganda. In
an age when a lot of technological advancements can
help in peddling untruths i.e....twitter, etc., we are on
the precipice of losing the exact definition of the word
truth.

One can actually put forward a lie or a far-fetched
conspiracy theory and if promoted well with sufficient
funds, it can become 'the truth' for a part of the electorate. This is shocking and disheartening. It should not
be happening in the world's most revered democracy.
Both sides understand and can agree to this.

In response to accusations against him for bribing
politicians, William A. Clark of Montana once said...
"I never bought a man that was not for sale." This

response is not a defense for what he did. But it certainly makes us wonder whether he would have been able to succeed in bribing those politicians if they had not been willing or predisposed to take the money in the first place.

The politicians and the political system at the time, created the atmosphere for such conduct to thrive.

This can be analogized to what is happening today. A political system that allows very wealthy individuals to funnel money into campaigns that they like, ad infinitum and without disclosure requirements, should make us wonder whether we are creating a political environment that is fertile for corruption.

Such political climates will potentially and inevitably lead to corruption. We might be replacing our democratic system with plutocracy, in which a rich few can get whatever they want by funding whomever they choose. We cannot let this happen. America is a meritocratic society that believes in democracy, not plutocracy or oligarchy.

To that end, elected officials of both parties should first find a way and pass laws that will essentially invalidate the Citizens United decision. It should no longer be a decision that applies in the political process because its relative advantages are far outweighed by the disadvantages.

Second, the Supreme Court should overturn the Citizens United decision. It should not be considered wrong when the court takes a second look at its decision and makes changes, if it is obvious that the first ruling is not achieving the desired objective. That, in my opinion, is encompassed in the doctrine of judicial review.

Third, there must be disclosure requirements for any campaign donation. Openness and accountability should be the centerpiece of an honest democratic process. Money corrupts. Excessive money corrupts excessively. Thus, details regarding campaign donations should be made public and brought to the light of day.

Furthermore, a candidate has to release information like tax returns, when demanded by the public. Releasing such information is very germane to the public discourse regarding that candidate and the prevailing issues at that time. A candidate can have transactions in their tax returns that may be legal, but not morally sound. A look into such a tax return will help the electorate in forming an opinion on the candidate's idiosyncrasies, visceral convictions and fiscal policies. This is necessary in determining how qualified that candidate can be for the position he is vying for.

Fourth, political ads have to contain the name of the candidate authorizing or approving the message. This is common sense. It ensures that there is accountability for the contents of an ad and will discourage super PACS from running ads with misleading messages, while the politician that it benefits claims that he was not aware of the contents of the advertisement.

Finally, there has to be caps on all campaign

contributions. There are caps already in place now. However, there should not be any exceptions. There should be caps on all donations.

In fact, having little money in campaigns epitomizes the right kind of democracy. Elections should not be sold to the highest bidder. Money should be less emphasized in an election. This will give way for a passionate and substantive debate on the issues that matter by the candidates.

Election absent passion equals a transaction. An election should always be a choice between two candidates and not a referendum on the incumbent. We should always try to elect politicians that are passionate and knowledgeable enough about the issues, to offer us a choice...a reason to hire them for the job instead of their opponent, and a reason to replace the incumbent.

Democrats and Republicans should therefore come together at all government levels and pass laws that will make these things possible. They should also enforce existing laws to that effect. If all these things are done, I am confident that our democracy would be right on track to continue as the most revered democracy in the world...a government of the people and for the people...a government with the consent of the governed, We the People.

4

IMMIGRATION

America is a nation of immigrants. Pretty much every family line that is here came from somewhere. The only difference is the time and the means or manner in which the different people came. We have to recognize this, ab initio, so that we can have a productive debate about fixing the problems in our immigration system, without treating the word *immigrant* as a pejorative word. There is nothing un-American about being an immigrant.

Legal immigration should be encouraged. This is because most people that come here legally jumped through a lot of hurdles in their home country's U.S. embassy, before obtaining the U.S. visa. They also pay a fee for the visa and related services. When they are already in the U.S., they work hard and continue to pay a lot of money to the immigration services, in order to change their status and become United States citizens.

I have a personal experience with this. I was a young man who came into this country with only $10 in my pocket and a burning desire to make it in this land of opportunity. I worked and went to law school and also became a U.S. citizen. A lot of legal immigrants have similar stories.

These people work hard and are disciplined. They pay taxes and are generally law abiding. They want to have a return on their investment because they know that they contribute in their own little ways to the greatness of this country.

America also benefits by having the best talents from other countries gravitating to the U.S. This is geopolitically and strategically advantageous for the country if we want to stay competitive in an increasingly globalized economy.

A legal immigrant can become an American citizen by naturalization and by adopting, believing and living under the principles of the American Idea. He can become quintessentially American by becoming patriotic, working hard, and abiding by the laws of the country based on the recognition that we are a nation of laws. Legal immigration should therefore be encouraged.

The true immigration problem in the country is illegal immigration. An illegal immigrant will likely be operating on a wrong premise which will inevitably lead to the wrong conclusion. It is harder to get to the right destination when one starts off in the wrong direction.

This is the problem facing our country today and our elected officials from both parties understand that. We therefore need a concerted effort by politicians on both sides of the aisle to stop all the demagoguery and divisive rhetoric and pass laws that focus mainly on discouraging illegal immigration and making legal immigration more attainable. Politicians should come together and agree on a comprehensive immigration reform. Some of the common sense measures are:

First, we have to secure our borders. This has to be done both as a matter of national security and as a matter of our sovereign or territorial integrity. The border should not be porous. We have to employ any means necessary, like increasing the security personnel, using more technology, etc. to ensure that the people and goods that enter into the country were authorized and sanctioned by the government. Prevention is better than cure. Tightening our borders will ensure that we do not constantly have the need to deport illegal immigrants. Deportation is not cost effective.

There are humane but firm ways to do this. Draconian laws and laws that are overly broad need not be used here. We have to use compassionate conservatism.

Second, we have to figure out how to effectively address the issue of the more that 11 million illegal immigrants by agreeing on programs that will enable them to come out of the shadows, begin on a path to adjust their status as lawful residents, openly enhance themselves and become more productive to the system. This is not amnesty. It is just a pragmatic approach to a problem that politicians do not like to talk about because they wish to avoid being perceived as either too soft or too hard on immigration.

The travesty here is that some people are under the delusion that we can easily deport the illegal immigrants that are currently in the country. The truth is that it is not financially feasible or even practical to round up and deport over 11 million people. It is impracticable.

Furthermore, the idea of training children in schools here in America and then deporting them later because they are not legal in the country, does not make sense. It is wasteful. There should be a way to put schoolchildren that benefit from the public education system on a path to citizenship so that they can use the skills and education obtained to work, pay taxes and strengthen our economy.

There is no easy way to do that without a lot of collateral damage and unforeseen consequences. We cannot put lipstick on this pig. We have to really think hard and carefully before separating families. The family is a microcosm of the larger nation. Family structures are necessary for a functioning society. Our politicians should therefore have this epiphany and level with the American people, so that this can be taken care of.

Third, we have to ensure that the illegal immigrants who continuously commit crimes, especially felonies, are sent back to their home countries permanently. This is because committing felonies in the U.S. simply indicates that the person does not really have any regard for the laws of the country.

Such measures will reduce crime and also reduce prison populations in states like Texas and California and insert a much needed distinction between the illegal immigrants that commit crimes and the illegal immigrants that only want to work hard to make life better for their families.

Fourth, we have to demagnetize the magnets in the states that attract illegal immigrants. What is it that makes a person from another country desire to migrate to a particular state? Perhaps employers are not strict on looking at the papers; maybe they just want cheap labor, etc.... Once such magnets are identified and demagnetized or made inoperative, their luster will be lost. Consequently, a potential illegal immigrant will think twice before choosing the place as an option to which to migrate.

Fifth, we have to enforce the laws that already exist in the books. There are a lot of codified laws regarding immigration that are not being adequately enforced. These laws have to be given teeth in order to actually achieve that which they were originally meant to achieve.

Finally, we have to encourage legal immigration

and pass laws that make it reasonably attainable for people who want to do it the right way. The red tape should be cut.

Legal immigration should be encouraged. It enhances America's strength and diversity. Diversity should be celebrated. What makes us different makes us stronger and more dynamic.

Look at the Olympics that recently took place in London and even at other Olympic games. Why did the U.S. beat every other country to rank first? It is because we have the most heterogeneous society...a melting pot where we have different people representing us in their areas of strength. Diversity is beautiful in America, the beautiful.

The U.S. also has professionals from different countries adopting the nation as their home, most notably Indian doctors and Asian engineers. America is a place where an Italian restaurant can be owned by a Hispanic, and a Mexican restaurant, owned and operated by Caucasians. This is remarkable.

You can hardly find this sort of amazing and unique phenomenon in any other country in the world. We ought to celebrate it because that is who we are as a nation—a country of immigrants with diverse races and ethnicities coming together and bringing all their dreams and abilities with them, to strengthen and enlarge the exceptional idea called America.

Our politicians and elected officials should celebrate this and pass laws that will implement these measures. They should enact and enforce immigration laws that show respect to individuals as human beings first.

This is in line with who we are as a nation…a nation of laws that respect the civil liberties of individuals, irrespective of where the person comes from.

5

REASONABLE FIREARMS RESTRAINTS

Following the shootings in Columbine, the shooting of Congresswoman Giffords, the Trayvon Martin shooting, the Aurora shootings and many more, any reasonable person in the country can agree that there is a need to place some sensible restrictions on the possession of firearms and ammunition.

I believe in the second amendment right to bear arms and that this right should be protected. However, both Democrats and Republicans understand and can agree that we have to ensure that the privilege to own a gun is conditioned on a strict background check and a serious evaluation of the potential gun owner.

We should not create a situation in which guns are brought to fistfights. As a former law enforcement officer in the state of Texas, I understand what it takes to use a gun responsibly. We cannot allow everybody to have easy access to guns and ammunition, and at the same time, expect a society where such privileges are not abused. Guns should be owned by people who can exercise good judgment under certain circumstances.

Anybody's child could have been watching a movie on the night of the shooting at the theatre in Aurora. The shooter was also able to buy a surprisingly large quantity of ammunition. Somebody should have noticed that something was amiss here. But nobody did and the tragedy occurred.

It would have been inconceivable even to the founding fathers, that the second amendment laws would make it possible that a shooter could have such access to the guns and large quantity of ammo that he had. Large numbers of people are dying every day in our cities and communities due to increased gun violence and gun-related crimes. Ironically, gun laws are growing increasingly relaxed across the states. This does not make a lot of sense.

Misguided application or interpretation takes away from the beauty of the second amendment right to bear arms. Thus to save and preserve these rights, we have to place necessary restrictions on gun ownership, so as to ensure that the second amendment continues to endure...as that symbol of American rugged individualism and independence from government.

Placing reasonable controls on gun ownership does not mean that the government wants to trample on the people's constitutional rights. The founding of this country was heralded by the sound of gun shots. We like guns. It is part of our cultural DNA and there is nothing wrong with that.

However, we have to ensure that we do not have a society where people who are unhinged have easy access to guns and large quantities of ammunition, as opposed to hardworking and law abiding citizens, who possess guns legitimately and use them responsibly for hunting and reasonable self-defense purposes. To that effect, politicians and lawmakers have to pass laws that will do the following:

First, there have to be serious physical and psychological evaluations of the potential gun owners. This is necessary in order to ensure that a person that applies for a license to own a gun is emotionally and mentally balanced.

Second, there has to be some reasonable restriction on the quantity of ammunition that an individual can make in one purchase.

Third, there should be a routine notification of law enforcement agencies for certain purchase amounts of ammunition and firearms. Common sense can be applied here. A gun seller may be able to suspect that certain purchases may not be used for the stated purpose. Under such circumstances, the seller should not hesitate to alert authorities regarding their suspicions.

Fourth, a detailed questionnaire and interview has to be conducted, concerning the purpose of the firearms and ammunition being purchased.

Fifth, we have to conduct an extensive background check on a potential gun owner. People that have committed certain crimes in the past should not get the license for gun ownership as people that have lived their lives in conformance with the requirements of the law.

Sixth, we should bring back the ban on high-capacity assault rifles. These guns are meant to be used by soldiers in a battlefield and have no place in the possession of private citizens. A deer does not need to receive numerous shots, in order for the hunter to establish the deer has been shot. There is also no need to continue firing at a potential aggressor in self defense when the threat of harm has been defused or is no longer imminent.

Finally, government should embark and promote programs designed to reorient and educate politicians and the electorate on the need for these restraints. These messaging and communications efforts will be helpful in clearing up the misinformation and disinformation that has plagued the reasonable restraints on firearms and ammunition in the country.

Politicians on both sides can agree to these measures. This should not be used as a wedge issue…everybody's children go to the movies. We are all vulnerable and are potential targets for the unhinged person with firearms and sufficient ammunition.

We ought to recognize this. It would be disingenuous

for our politicians and elected officials to pretend as if these solutions are not obvious. They should therefore pass common sense laws that can implement these measures. Failure to do this is not acceptable.

To the souls of the innocent that die from such gun incidents, we as a society will have failed them, if we do not enact and enforce laws that will drastically reduce these tragedies.

We are better than that.

6

JOB CREATION

Jobs are necessary for the economy to grow. Employment ensures upward mobility for individuals and families within the country. In addition to the provision of means of livelihood, it also restores and preserves the dignity of mankind.

For a lot of people, happiness and human dignity are tied to their jobs or careers and the satisfaction or self-worth that they derive from such jobs. In the coming election, economy is the issue that is the most cogent in people's minds. Economic strength is achieved in the country when there is abundance of jobs for anybody that wants to work.

An abundance of jobs leads to a lower unemployment rate which invariably leads to less dependence on government aid and welfare services. Economic strength even impacts our military strength. An economically strong nation will likely be a militarily strong nation and vice versa. It is all related. The importance of job creation can therefore never be overemphasized. It should always be a top priority for elected officials on both sides.

Recently, politicians on both sides have been unnecessarily doctrinaire on this issue. Republicans seriously advocate the concept of supply side economics. This concept basically represents trickle-down economics, in which a select few that are regarded as job creators should be given all the tax breaks and be totally encouraged financially, in the hope that they will do well and create more jobs that will benefit the country.

They believe in the free market and deregulation. They believe that regulation from government chills the entrepreneurial spirit of the American businessman. They would prefer the market to self-regulate.

Democrats, on the other hand, believe that the economy is strengthened if the government intervenes in the marketplace by making policies that will benefit the average citizen and serve as a means of upward mobility for the poor and the middle class. They believe that government has a role in regulating the markets, creating jobs and leveling the playing field so that everybody can have a fair chance at getting a job and providing for their families. This is keynesian economics.

Both sides are unnecessarily critical of the other. Republicans think the Democrats practice statism and encourage dependence on government programs. Democrats feel that the Republicans want deregulation and plutocracy to be the order of the day.

These conflicting philosophies and perspectives are actually a big part of what is keeping politicians and elected officials from coming together to adopt policies that will actually provide the right atmosphere for increased job creation. This trend has to stop so that we can be able to create more jobs and strengthen the economy.

Both sides have a point, but there is a happy medium somewhere in the middle. The truth is that most jobs are typically created in the private sector. That is fundamental in our capitalist system. Less government is good so that there is less encroachment on individual freedoms. Government policies should not foster a culture of dependency and collectivism among its citizens.

Success and individual accomplishments should be celebrated and not attacked. That is the American spirit. It is this entrepreneurial and innovative state of mind that unleashes creativity and provides the atmosphere necessary for job creation.

It is this mindset of rugged individualism that makes Americans, including the middle class, the most formidable economic machine in the world.

On the other hand, government's role should not be dismissed. It has an important role. It is there to do for individuals what they cannot do for themselves. Regulations in the markets are necessary. Laissez faire capitalism, only, may not work. Government should be there to provide rules, regulations and restraints in society in order to avoid social Darwinism. Rugged individualism should be encouraged, but not to the detriment of certain disadvantaged people in the society.

Self-preservation may be the first law of nature, but that is premised on the assumption that human beings are still in the jungle. We cannot function as if we live in the 'wild, wild West' or without civilization. Survival of the fittest should not be the order of the day. The human race has evolved.

A society has an obligation to aid the disadvantaged and most vulnerable to ensure that they get a fair shot in achievement and job opportunities. Compassionate conservative measures should be adopted, so as to give the disadvantaged a fighting chance.

Given all of these self-evident truths, politicians and elected officials should come together and agree on these moderate views instead of sticking to the traditional ideologies of their parties. When they do this, they will be able to pass meaningful legislation that will implement these job-creating measures.

First, there should not be excessive regulations on any industry or business. This is because overregulation reduces the rate of job creation by making the businessman spend too much trying to be in compliance with the rules, instead of hiring more workers. Regulation should be necessary, targeted and unambiguous.

Such focused regulations will also remove uncertainties and make an investor more amenable to investing in the economy, as opposed to merely saving his or her money.

Second, government should discourage outsourcing of jobs to countries like China and India. It should encourage insourcing by incentivizing companies that stay here in America and hire American workers to do the work needed. More products should be stamped with the three proud words: Made in America.

Third, worker unions that protect the rights of the worker, like fair wages, should be encouraged. The unions that are overly politicized or involve themselves in activities that do not directly benefit and protect the worker's rights should be dissolved. Fair wage practices should be the norm everywhere. A person should be able to get a fair wage for any work done. This will incentivize and motivate people to work, if they know that they are being fairly paid and their rights will be adequately safeguarded.

Fourth, government should also make business loans more easily obtainable. This will remove the red tape and bureaucracy associated with obtaining such loans and will make it easier for start-ups to thrive.

The government should also look into rebuilding infrastructures in the country. Statistics show that there are a lot of old bridges in the country that will need to be rebuilt. There should be no delay in starting construction projects aimed at rebuilding these bridges and some roads.

Finally, politicians and elected officials should reassess past job bills that were disapproved, to determine if they were disapproved for the right reasons, or just for political reasons. Such job bills should be analyzed once again and approved, if they are found to be economically feasible.

These measures can be agreed on by both sides. It is the reasonable thing to do. If politicians from both parties adopt policies that will implement these measures, then they would have done their part in helping to create more jobs, and put the country on a path towards economic stability and fiscal discipline.

7

THE U.S. SUPREME COURT

The United States Supreme Court is the most powerful and revered judicial institution in the world. It has the last word on any issue in the country. Its interpretation of the Constitution constitutes the supreme law of the land. It also has the judicial review power with which to invalidate state laws that are inconsistent with the U.S. Constitution.

However, this institution has also been having some image problems. Its approval rating is at an all-time low. Following controversial decisions in Bush v. Gore and Citizens United cases, it became really imperative that the Supreme Court give a ruling that could be perceived as non-partisan. They did just that by upholding the Affordable Care Act. They were able to wade through all the misinformation and disinformation that surrounded the health care bill to reach a reasonable conclusion. This was a great redemption to its image. It is a step in the right direction.

The main problem with the Supreme Court is that in recent years, their rulings were perceived to be exceptionally partisan. It seems like the rulings are not conclusions reached by impartial, non-partisan legal luminaries that can disagree without being disagreeable.

Citizens United has been the most consequential decision. It has opened up the floodgates of huge amounts of money being funneled into the political system. The ruling essentially held that corporations are people and should be allowed to spend freely in an election. It equated money with speech.

The problem with this notion is that if money is the same as speech, then the rich will invariably have more publicized freedom of speech. The playing field will not be level because the voice of the little guy is stifled and not heard. This is not good for our democracy and our first amendment rights.

The Supreme Court justices represent our best and brightest and are expected to be above politics, but this notion is not very clear now. This is an honorable institution and is a vital part of the government. Elected officials should therefore easily agree and pass laws that will solve these image problems very quickly.

Some of the measures are:

First, removal of life tenures for the Supreme Court Justices and putting term limits on their positions. The reason for them to serve for life is so that they cannot be afraid of the political repercussions of their rulings and can thus be above politics.

However, this idea seems like an oxymoron when juxtaposed with the practice of having presidents of particular parties appoint them. A president from a particular party appoints a Justice to help further the president's agenda and policies. That, by its nature, is a political move. Thus it is almost inescapable for them not to be influenced by politics on some level.

Second, eligible people for the positions should be elected and not appointed. They should pass through the Democratic process so that they will feel it in their souls that they have a mandate...an obligation, to rule according to the will of the people and not feel unnecessarily loyal to the president that appointed them.

Third, the court has to overturn the Citizens United decision. The court should be able to address an obviously faulty ruling and still retain its credibility. In fact, the court becomes more respectable if it shows that it is an institution that is willing to self-correct, instead of just sticking to precedent that translates into bad policies.

Democrats and Republicans ought to have a conversation about these measures. Chief Justice Roberts is a reasonable and pragmatic jurist and elected officials will find in him, a visionary leader who wants to redirect the trajectory of the image of the Supreme Court to its highest possible height.

8

HEALTHCARE

The health care problem has bothered the country for a while now. Everybody knew that it needed to be fixed but there was not bipartisan cooperation to pass laws that will cover everybody. Senator Ted Kennedy fought to have this, but could not achieve it before he died.

We spend the most in healthcare but do not get the best care when compared to other industrialized nations. It surely makes sense that we make laws that will be geared toward giving universal healthcare to all American citizens. Healthcare ought to be a right, not a privilege. I have heard people argue against that but the truth is that we still end up spending the taxpayers' dollars to take care of the uninsured when they are injured.

It was estimated that about $250 million was spent on negative ads against the Affordable Care Act.

This is why the popularity of the law did not poll well. Such negative ads with that huge amount of money are not good for our democracy. This is because they have the capacity to change minds and mislead people through disinformation, misinformation and distortion of facts.

The simple solution to this problem is to fully adopt and implement the provisions of the Affordable Care Act, signed into law by President Obama. Challenges to this law have also reached the Supreme Court. The Supreme Court under Chief Justice Roberts upheld the law.

Thus, the Affordable Care Act is the law of the land. This is a law that was modeled after the healthcare law in Massachusetts signed into law by the governor at the time, Mitt Romney. The Affordable Care Act has numerous advantages. The most significant, however, is that insurance companies will no longer deny coverage to some people based on pre-existing conditions. It will also reduce the cost of healthcare over the years and improve the care received, while eliminating waste and the inefficiencies that burden the healthcare system.

The politicians that always oppose it should therefore stop and embrace the program because it is the law of the land. It is not perfect, but we should always continue to perfect it. Elected officials should come together and figure out what they would like to change, but also propose sensible and viable alternatives.

Otherwise, anything else will be demagoguery and the unnecessary jingoistic conduct that excites ideologues. America does not want that now.

America stands to benefit more from the Affordable Care Act if it is implemented completely and efficiently.

9

CONGRESS

Congress represents the legislative branch of the government. It currently has the lowest job approval rating that it has ever had. This is because congressmen and women have become increasingly partisan. Their motto is...party before country.

This practice has to stop in order for us to see meaningful accomplishments. The practice has to be... country before party. The representatives and politicians have to listen to the people and not to their donors. There has been evidence that some politicians now spend more time seeking money than actually doing their jobs.

This is part of the problem caused by the Citizens United decision. These politicians are beholden to the people who donate money to their campaigns, rather than to their own constituents. This affects the nature of our democracy. The first words in the United States Constitution are "We the People," and they are there for a reason. Abraham Lincoln defined democracy as government of the people, by the people, and for the people.

We, as a nation, must keep it that way in order to safeguard our cherished democracy. In recent years, due to the gridlock in Congress, the U.S. credit rating was downgraded. There has been opposition to whatever the Obama administration proposed. Even the judicial branch, which is supposed to be above politics, is sometimes dragged into the mud fight of this gridlock. Separation of powers is not as sacred as it ought to be.

Everybody agrees that the economic problems facing the country can be solved by growing the economy, balancing the budget and raising revenue. If spending is done under a balanced budget, then the deficit will be reduced, because we will not be spending money that we do not have.

The idea of fiscal conservatism is very important. Unfortunately, many people use the phrase without really understanding the concept. Simply stated, it means spending money wisely. Families do that. We all do that in our private lives. We budget. We often limit spending and make necessary cuts, to be able to function in a given situation. Government should do that too.

Congress should audit agencies and close down loopholes. Government agencies have to be lean and efficient. They have to be frugal. The question should always be...if money is being spent on something, what are the benefits being derived from it? We cannot continue the excessive consumer culture and still expect to have a surplus.

An economy where we borrow more than the revenue we create is not sustainable in the long run. The angst regarding the economy should not be there, if elected officials from both sides of the aisle do what they are supposed to do.

Surplus can be realized when there is more revenue than what the government spends. Thus, there should be no sacred cows when it comes to departments and agencies that need to receive cuts. Such cuts, however, should not be done arbitrarily. They should be surgical enough to prevent waste at the point needed, but not so broad as to paralyze the institution. That would mean cutting off the nose to spite the face. Cuts should be sensible and targeted.

For instance, programs like Medicare or Social Security are not going to be sustainable, and there has to be a consensus on solving these problems. Congress should not waste time pursuing policies that do not help the country, like voter ID laws. Voting should be expanded. Such voter ID laws should not be encouraged. This is a solution looking for a problem. Statistics show that incidents of voter fraud are so negligible or non-existent, as to not warrant the codification of laws that will limit people's voting rights.

Voting is a right, not a privilege and the notion of allowing everybody to participate in elections is vital to the sustenance of our democracy. We should be more inclusive as opposed to being exclusive. Abolishing such laws will eliminate electoral dysfunction and ensure that no person is disenfranchised or unduly denied from participation in our democracy.

This should be obvious to members of congress and should remind them not to pursue policies that do not really solve the country's problems.

Congress is one of the three branches of government. These branches are supposed to be coequal branches, functioning as checks and balances to one another without undermining any one branch. However, that is currently not the case. We have to return the system to what the founding fathers intended it to be – three branches of government working together in good faith and with the best interests of the American people at heart.

To that end, we should first stop politicians from receiving money and campaign donations from lobbyist groups. When lobbyists pay into a campaign, they expect something in return. I have yet to see a lobbyist group that lobbies for the interests of the common man. This sort of quid pro quo should be discouraged.

Campaigns should be funded at the grassroots level by donations from the people to be governed. The little private donation is in itself a form of endorsement or acceptance of that leader. It shows better acceptance by regular people and this is the essence of democracy.

Individuals or groups simply should not be able to write big checks to campaigns. This is because the cost of such payments is ultimately borne by the masses.

Second, the adversarial and competitive nature in which congress conducts its activities should be discouraged. The pugilistic attitude that is prevalent in our politics now, should not be encouraged. Democrats and Republicans are not opponents and should not be fighting with a 'winner takes all' mentality. They should work as two parties that may have divergent views or approaches to solving the nation's problems.

They should always be united by love of country and a burning desire to solve problems for the people who gave them the opportunity to serve.

Third... respect, congeniality and decency should be returned to our political discourse. There is no need for hyperbolic epithets to be used to vilify another politician with whom we disagree on policy. There has to be a paradigm shift in the manner with which we discuss politics in this country. We can disagree without being disagreeable. Decent and respectful political discourse will prevent untruths and distortion of facts and will also elevate our politics.

Fourth, there should be rules in congress that make a politician retract or correct a statement they put out that is shown to be significantly and factually inaccurate. Fact checkers have a role. Facts and truth should matter in our politics to prevent misinformation and disinformation. The use of facts should be promoted in our political discourse and not the use of factoids. Politicians and elected officials should be held accountable when they engage in obvious selective amnesia regarding their position on issues. They ought to say what they mean and mean what they say. Anything short of this is tantamount to a willful deception of voters. Such practices have an attenuating effect on our vibrant democracy. A knowledgeable electorate is vital for the sustenance of any democracy.

Fifth, there should be serious limits placed on the time that elected officials spend on fund raising as opposed to actually doing their jobs. Politicians should strive to be statesmen and not just ordinary politicians who are always focused on how to win during the next election cycle. Their time should be spent more on making policies. Once the policy is done correctly, politics will take care of itself.

If these things are done by the leaders of both parties, it would be a significant step in restoring the dignity and reputation that congress once had. It will also make the world's most revered legislative institution seem once again like an arena where ideas are fought over, honorably - by intellectual giants and gymnasts engaging in very heated debates.

Congress will once again be the citadel of happy warriors who are willing to engage in complex debates designed to hash out the best solution to any problem that the country is facing. It will be an institution that will truly be occupied by the best and brightest in our society.

10

DEATH PENALTY

America remains one of the few industrialized countries that still give death penalty sentences to offenders for certain crimes. There are many arguments for and against the death penalty. However, I think that this is an area in which there should be uniformity of practice among the states. We should either be a country that allows death penalty sentences or not.

Currently, some states have it and some do not. States like Texas have a lot of death row inmates and are proud to lead the country in execution numbers. This is a situation where our elected officials and politicians have to act fast and reasonably, to determine the direction the country ought to go.

Traditionally, Republicans or conservatives tend to be ok with the death penalty while the Democrats or progressives tend not to be comfortable with it. This should not be a partisan issue. It is an issue that people feel deep inside their hearts.

I believe that we as a society should be tough on crimes and we should adequately punish heinous crimes. Punishment serves as a deterrent to a potential criminal. If he understands that he may be executed for committing a crime, he might just think twice before committing such crimes of depravity or moral turpitude.

Conversely, if a potential criminal believes that the most he can get is a prison sentence and that he may even lessen the sentence with good behavior in prison, he may not be discouraged enough to avoid committing such crimes. This is just human nature. I have worked in law enforcement in Texas and I have seen firsthand that some prisoners really do not have a problem doing prison time. That is why we have a high rate of recidivism in the system.

Prisoners in the U.S. are well fed, watch TV, engage in a lot of recreational activities and even celebrate most holidays. This is so because, at the core, we are a compassionate people and will not imprison criminals in inhumane conditions. This is a good thing; however, it may not be able to deter some crimes. Thus, death penalty sentences become really necessary in a humane society such as ours.

Furthermore, in the case of a cold-blooded murder, the death penalty affords the victim's family some sort of redress and makes them not to look for self-help in order to revenge or avenge the death of their loved one. State supervised execution in a case like this can serve as vengeance, which can be therapeutic in this kind of situation. It may not bring back the dead victim, but it alleviates the pain and reduces the feeling of powerlessness that the victim's family experiences.

I cannot imagine the disgusting feeling that a father would feel if he learns that a criminal who had brutally raped and murdered his only daughter is out on parole. It is not fair or right. Justice in such cases has to be served swiftly and adequately by the government.

On the other hand, I have also heard that such death penalty programs are controversial and are not very evolved. These problems are self-evident. There are also situations in which executions are botched and not done in an effective manner, causing them to be unnecessarily expensive and inhumane.

Sometimes they are conducted using methods that run afoul of the eighth amendment provisions against cruel and unusual punishment. Death row inmates also tend to violate prison rules and endanger the safety of the officers and other inmates with impunity. This is because they do not have anything at stake.

These problems can be solved by the elected officials if they can come together and pass laws and policies that are reasonable, sensible and address most of the concerns raised.

To that end, we should first decide whether or not we want to continue death penalty sentences as a country. If we are not to continue, then the cases against all death row inmates should be reassessed to determine the appropriate punishment for the particular crime committed.

Second, if we are to continue, we have to ensure that adequate due process protections are given to such offenders and that the sentences are clear and decisive. We have to make sure that such sentences are reserved for crimes that are so barbaric and depraved that even the offenders can admit that they deserve the death penalty.

Third, fast and modern techniques should be used for the executions, to ensure that they are humane and that the offender does not suffer unnecessarily before dying.

Our politicians and elected officials can come together on these centrist solutions by passing laws and policies that will make this a reality. These policies will also save a lot of money for the taxpayers and will decrease the overcrowded prison populations across the country.

We have to always be conscious of due process and the constitutional requirements against cruel and unusual punishment. This will show that we are a civilized country that does not savor the 'blood sport' of executions, but a nation of laws where justice gets delivered to deserving individuals, in a fair and decisive manner.

EPILOGUE

Having gone through some of our monumental problems and the pragmatic solutions that would help in
solving them, it should be noted that this list is not
exhaustive of all the issues that affect this country. This
American union may not be perfect, but we cannot
stop trying to perfect it.

There are other things that could be done. However,
we cannot let our quest for perfection be the enemy of
good. A completely egalitarian society may not be achiev-
able, but we have to at least strive to make it fair. The
gravamen of the proposition in this book is that we have
to start from somewhere in trying to solve our problems.
That place is at the middle…the confluence point.

We have to start applying common-sense, centric
approaches to solving these problems. It is pusillani-
mous for us to continue delaying. The time is now. We

are who we are waiting for. We have a moral obligation to pull our government out from the nadir to which it may be headed, by removing the gridlock in our politics.

We should always remember the words of Franklin Delano Roosevelt... Competition has been shown to be useful up to a certain point and no further, but cooperation, which is the thing we must strive for today, begins where competition leaves off.

These words were right then and are right in our present political state. Our politics should not be only about competition, but also cooperation.

Huberus in politicians and elected officials should not be rewarded. Unnecessary competition between the parties should not be encouraged. Politics ought to be about the good of the country, not the politicians themselves. Elected officials should not be intellectually dishonest when discussing important national issues.

Our politicians have to understand that even when they campaign with poetry, they still have to govern with prose. This means that the proper execution of the jobs for which they were elected should be top priority in relation to the lofty campaign speeches.

Execution of the job requires compromise, a word that must be embedded in our political lexicon. The absence of compromise has real consequences. For instance, it led to the downgrading of the U.S. credit rating for the first time, a few years ago. Politicians are elected to do deals. That is in their job descriptions.

They are not paid to be the bastion or the vanguard of extreme ideologies. Faith and social issues have to be deemphasized in our politics. We have churches for that. In a president, we prefer a commander in chief, not a preacher in chief. This is in line with the concept of separation of church and state. The electorate has to demand this, and a politician that is not doing that is simply showing insubordination to the employer.

Such a politician ought to be fired...voted out of office by the electorate.

I believe in the dynamism of the American people and I prognosticate that if compromise and solution-oriented approaches are adopted by our politicians and elected officials, America will be on its way to overcoming most of its setbacks, reviving the economy and will continue to be the best hope of humanity on earth.

America will continue to be the place where everybody will always long to come to, from sea to shining sea.

ABOUT THE AUTHOR

Ralph E. Nwobi is an American author, law school graduate, political analyst and commentator. He is a U.S. citizen, originally born in Nigeria. His religious preference is Catholicism. In this book Ralph also draws from his past experiences as a teacher, law enforcement officer and a chemist. These divergent fields of endeavor make him uniquely qualified to bring a multi-faceted and analytical approach to solving our most enduring national challenges.

Ralph became interested in politics and government policies at an early stage in life. He is a conservative Democrat and currently resides in Sacramento, California.